HOW TO WRITE SEX

(ADVICE TO AUTHORS)

BY HELEN COX

Copyright © 2020 by Helen Cox.
Published in the United Kingdom by Helen Cox Books.

Ebook ISBN: 978-1-8380221-9-8
Paperback ISBN: 978-1-8380801-3-6
Hardback ISBN: 978-1-8380801-4-3

No part of this book may be used or reproduced in any manner whatsoever without written permission except in the case of brief quotations embodied in critical articles or reviews. For further information, visit helencoxbooks.com.

Helen Cox is a Yorkshire-born novelist and poet. She holds an MA in Literature and Creative Writing from the University of York St John and has taught creative writing for a decade. During her prolific writing career, Helen has written sensual romance, steamy romance and romantic mystery novels, which have been published by both HarperCollins and Quercus Books. She currently lives by the sea in Sunderland and spends an inordinate amount of time photographing local lighthouses. You can find out more about Helen's work at HelenCoxBooks.Com

ADVICE TO AUTHORS SERIES

How and When to Sign a Book Deal

How to Become a Published Writer

How to Write Page-Turning Fiction

How and When to Quit Your Day Job

Contents

INTRODUCTION: SHAME, SHAME,
WE KNOW YOUR NAME 5

Chapter 1.	SEX POSITIVITY 13
Chapter 2.	THE MOST IMPORTANT SEXUAL ORGAN 20
Chapter 3.	CONSENT 26
Chapter 4.	HEAT LEVELS 36
Chapter 5.	NAUGHTY WORDS AND HOW TO USE THEM 44
Chapter 6.	SETTING THE MOOD 51
Chapter 7.	MEANINGFUL SEX 57
Chapter 8.	WHAT IS SEXY? 63
Chapter 9.	REWRITING SEX 70
Chapter 10.	WORKING WITH THE SENSES . . 75
Chapter 11.	THE ROLE OF SETTING 82
Chapter 12.	ARE PENNAMES WORTH IT? . . . 87

Author's Note 95
Further Reading and Resources 96
Acknowledgements 97

INTRODUCTION: SHAME, SHAME, WE KNOW YOUR NAME

The first obstacle that any writer must overleap when they take the decision to write about sex is that of shame. You know what I'm talking about: the sinking feeling you get in your stomach when you think about people reading those saucy passages you penned on a Friday commute home from the office. The vignettes you wrote when you felt frivolous and bold at the mere idea of the weekend being nigh.

Oh come on, I can't be alone on this?

Those of you who have already given this line of writing some thought may have started to get to grips with, what is for many writers, the biggest single deterrent to exploring physical intimacy on the page. Others however may have secretly ordered this book to their e-reader or hidden their paperback edition from their family when it arrived in the post. Both are understandable reactions and unfortunately are born of centuries of shaming when it comes to discussing and engaging in sexual contact.

Many authors are simply too afraid to explore this aspect of relationships in what feels like a very public space. Often, this fear stems from the readers' tendency to conflate a writer with their characters. 'But I've written a book about an Egyptian Explorer in the 1930s,' we cry 'and I'm not an Egyptian Explorer in the 1930s.'

No matter how much we protest that we are not our characters and that what we present is an outrageously twisted version of reality as we know it, readers do tend to assume that an author is writing from personal experience. 'But what part of this work is based on your life?' readers call back.

To which, we respond with a sigh and pour ourselves a stiff lemonade.

Sometimes, though we are just trying to tell an engaging story in one hundred thousand words or fewer, readers seem desperate to decode our psychology through the strange situations we present. And, if we're honest, some of our own quirks or thoughts or feelings or ideas are likely to get worked in to stories we write. But fiction is not autobiography. The inclination of our readers to mistake one for the other is often what prevents writers from exploring sexual content, for fear the reader will assume that we are laying bare our own sexual preferences and desires for all to see. Or perhaps even describing a sexual experience we have had verbatim while hiding behind the mask of fiction. I'm sure some writers may have done this, but due to the fact that real life as it stands rarely makes for good fiction, I would say it was much less common that readers suspect.

This problem is exacerbated when writers consider that people they know may read what they write. Thinking about our mothers, fathers, sisters, aunties and friends reading our rendering of intimate moments in black and white, well, for many of us that idea isn't exactly a turn-on. And this is an issue that every writer who attempts to capture intimacy on the page must grapple with. Whatever embarrassment you feel over this I think it's important to establish a core scientific truth about the act of sexual intercourse.

By our very existence, almost all of us have a connection to sexual relationships. Sexual contact is, more often than not, the context for the life we have been given. Even for those of us who have been conceived via IVF treatment, sexual contact played a part in that story. It was very likely the first go-to for your parents when they were trying to conceive. If you had a single mother or if your parents are a same-sex couple, they will likely have paid a heavy price for the joy of bringing you into the world because they couldn't conceive a child in what is traditionally known as 'the natural way.'

And it's very important that we dwell on that word natural.

Because when we're talking about the conception of a child we're more than happy to frame sexual relationships as natural. When it comes to a conversation about pleasure or hedonism however, sexual contact so often becomes a topic of humiliation, ridicule and control. At best, puerile humour is used to avoid addressing the real points we need to discuss when it comes to this area of our lives.

I put it to you, in this introductory chapter, that sexual contact should not be a source of humiliation. That we all have a connection to sexual relationships and that fact alone makes it a natural and wonderful part of our lives. By allowing others with narrow views of the subject limit what you are willing to explore in your writing, you not only prevent yourself from exploring the depth at which you can describe relationships but you also short change your reader.

Being physically intimate with a person and sharing our desires is for many a wholeheartedly frightening thing to do. Moreover, not everyone has the confidence or the option to explore their sexuality in person. Consequently many turn to erotic literature to find out more about this most private part of who they are. To safely explore where the limits lie. To find out if there are experiences they haven't tried that they might enjoy. To indulge a fantasy that they would never want to act out but that sets their heart racing when they think about it. Perhaps most importantly, to know from the outset via literary exploration what they absolutely do not want when they close the bedroom door.

Allowing readers to explore their fantasies and dreams enables them to make more considered choices about their real sex life. In short, work such as this may build a bridge between the reader and profound sexual fulfilment. Which is a pretty awesome thing to help someone achieve.

Still have reservations? Still convinced it is just too scary a prospect to put pen to paper in this way? Let me share with you the opening lines to the poem Dildoides by Samuel Butler. It was written in 1672 as a lament over the public burning of dildos in Stocksmarket.

Dildoides

Such a sad tale prepare to hear,
As claims from either sex a tear.
Twelve dildoes meant for the support
Of aged lechers of the Court
Were lately burnt by impious hand
Of trading rascals of the land,
Who envying their curious frame,
Expos'd those Priaps to the flame.
Oh! Barbarous times! when deities
Are made themselves a sacriice!
Some were composed of shining horns,
More precious than the unicorn's.
Some were of wax, where ev'ry vein,
And smallest ibre were made plain.
Some were for tender virgins it,
Some for the large fallacious slit
Of a rank lady, tho' so torn,
She hardly feels when child is born.

The reason I'm showing you this work, which appears alongside many other examples of sex writing in *The Literary Companion to Sex* edited by Fiona Pitt-Kethley, is because I know that if you are a writer suffering from trepidation at the prospect of writing sex, you'll likely have some notion that you are doing something outrageously new, scary and taboo. I hate to be the one to break it to you (not really, I love being the one to break it to you) but pretty much any smutty thing we can dream up was more than likely committed to the page centuries ago. Take a brief skim of the Kama Sutra and you'll have all the evidence you need that writing vividly about sex is nothing fresh or radical.

Because we like to think of ourselves as deeply original when compared with past generations, we tend to think of pornography and the erotic as something that we invented, shortly after we invented the internet. In truth, people have been interested in sexually charged texts almost since writing began. Sex is a great mystery and what better way to understand it than read about – or watch – consenting adults participating in it? The extract on the previous page is evidence of our long-running obsession with the sexual. It is also evidence in support of the argument that you will have to go a long way to top the explicit nature of the writers who wrote before you.

Thus, if Samuel Butler can lament the public burning of dildos in 1672, I think that you, dear reader, can write an explicit sex scene between your characters in the 21st Century with little trouble. If you want to throw a bit of dildo burning into the mix, by all means be my guest.

Just remember to credit Butler for the inspiration.

CHAPTER ONE:

SEX POSITIVITY

Should you have read this far, despite the threat of nigh on crippling shame, and still wish to write about sexual relationships, I recommend that you become an immediate advocate of the Sex Positive Movement. Don't worry, there's no weird initiation ritual, well, at least not as far as I know. But researching this movement and interacting with like-minded folks is one of swiftest methods of claiming your right to explore sexual experiences in your stories and poems. Moreover, embracing a sex positive perspective will support you in claiming that right without carrying shame, guilt or embarrassment around with you.

Sex positivity is a broad church. Like any movement, there is no one definition that fits all who subscribe to it. On the whole however, it can be defined as a social movement that celebrates all manner of sexual unions, so long as everyone involved is a consenting adult. Some might also add the stipulation that the acts performed cannot be illegal but of course it depends where in the world you live as to how viable that is. The rules about sexual conduct are much stricter in some places than in others and thus not everybody applies this condition.

Why is the sex positivity movement even necessary? Shouldn't we all just agree that what people get up to behind closed doors is their own business? If only! Views about sexuality in Western society are still largely dictated by a historical hangover created by our inability to completely let go of Victorian societal norms. Many in modern society think themselves super liberal, and some of them are, but there is still an undercurrent of this unfortunate element of Victoriana embedded in the stories we tell about sex – one only has to look at the headlines in certain newspapers to verify this.

It wasn't always like this. When it came to how we viewed the human enjoyment of sex, the Western world did at least start out on a more sex positive track. Societal ideas were still grossly heteronormative, and thus limiting for many individuals who didn't identify as heterosexual, but at least pleasure played a part in the accepted view of sexual intercourse. Between the time in which the Greeks reigned supreme and the Elizabethan era, it was believed that during intercourse, both the man and the woman needed to reach an orgasm in order to produce a child. After this period however, thinking began to change and not, to my mind, for the better.

After this point, sexual contact was to be entered into only for the pious purpose of making a baby. The pressure for a husband to provide his wife with an orgasm was – er – relieved and passed on to his wife's doctor who, yes, honestly, took the liberty of stimulating many of their female patients to orgasm until the invention of the vibrator... Oh sorry, no. It was actually described as a neck massager. Such was the shame that surrounded the female orgasm. This denial of female sexual pleasure, of course, hasn't ceased in modern times as we read far too regularly about female genital mutilation, a practice inflicted to blunt the sexual urge in women.

In addition to the above less-than-inspiring potted history of the orgasm, for many centuries people, but particularly women, who had sex before marriage suffered huge reputational damage. If a lady 'indulged' herself in this manner, social rules dictated they would be considered a fallen woman, damaged goods and no longer marriage material. This was a bit of a bind to be in when women were not permitted to handle financial matters. If women did marry, and the majority did if not out of love then out of necessity, it was also largely agreed that women should submit to the sexual desires of their husband and should consider themselves under their husband's sexual control.

We still struggle with some of these Victorian ideas today. So many of our beliefs - and media - surrounding sexual intimacy even now revolve around categorising people in certain out-dated terms: the prude; the stud; the slut, the list goes on. Such words and ideas continue to be used - or more modern versions of them - to define people and their relationship to sexual intercourse, and also to control how they access that part of themselves.

Perhaps the biggest problem with such categories is that they are restrictive, they are limiting and derogatory. They position sexual relationships as a filthy secret that should be hidden and never publicly talked about or explored. It's thinking such as this that led to boys over the centuries being told that masturbation created all manner of ills – most commonly blindness – while it was simultaneously assumed little girls did not engage in such 'dirty habits'.

As you may have guessed by the phrase 'sex positivity', this movement is about redefining sexual relationships in more positive terms. And not just heteronormative, vanilla sexual relationships but all kinds so long as everyone involved is consenting and of age.

Sex positivity champions the idea that sexual activity is just another way for human beings to express themselves. That there is no shame attached to the act, even if people engage in deeply kinky fetishes. Many a subscriber to sex positive ideals believes that ignoring or trying to suppress our deepest sexual urges rather than accept and acknowledge them can have a dark psychological impact on a person.

Conversely, advocates of sex positivity assume many benefits to embracing and exploring our sexual preferences without inhibition. These include the opportunity to understand ourselves and our place in the world even better than we might otherwise; the ability to renew our self-esteem; the confidence to take charge of our sexuality and the required acumen to redefine and reclaim old damaging insults designed to limit our sexual experience and the ways in which we are permitted to sexually connect with others. Through role play, sexual experimentation is even believed to help heal old wounds inflicted by abusers as participants have the opportunity to script their own bedroom scene and regain the control in this setting. In short, the favourable outcomes to positive participation in sexual experiences are numerous and thus worthy of inclusion in our stories and poems.

When I write stories, regardless of what kind of story I'm writing, it is important to me that the reader understands I embrace a sex positive perspective. My characters talk about sex openly, it is not something to be swept under the carpet or hidden. It is something to be celebrated and enjoyed. It is just a natural part of life. For, so long as the necessary precautions are taken to prevent disease and protect a woman from an unplanned pregnancy, what possible harm can come from two people consenting to be intimate with each other in ways that perhaps they've never consented to being intimate with anyone else?

And this keyword intimacy is something that is that the heart of writing sex. If you want to engage your reader with the steamier scenes you have composed, you need to go beyond describing the physical stimulation your characters feel. Every intimate scene, in fact arguably every scene whether it's intimate or not, needs an emotional core. This doesn't mean that the people you are writing about have to fall madly in love with each other. The emotion you're grappling with might not be an admirable one. It might be a desire for validation, or revenge or physical dominance. Even if your characters are just lonely and in an amorous mood however, casual sex can still be meaningful and respectful.

Especially if we show people how by modelling it through our characters.

Assuming a sex positive perspective when writing intimate scenes means positioning yourself as an artist painting a portrait of the scene unfolding and the people playing a part within it. Your characters might be into some deeply risky sex games that you would never for a second consider engaging in yourself. Your characters may be making some terrible relationship decisions that a more sensible person would not. But it's important that the writer doesn't judge her characters. Instead, our job is to show our readers what it is about that sexual practice or encounter that has a lasting impact on the players and their journey. What is different about this sexual encounter when compared to the encounters they've had before? Which emotional and psychological buttons is the partner (or partners) they're engaging with pushing and how are they making this happen?

Which leads us on to a very important question that all writers delving into intimate material need to be sure of the answer to: do you know what the most important sexual organ is?

CHAPTER TWO:

THE MOST IMPORTANT SEXUAL ORGAN

Contrary popular belief, the most important sexual organ cannot be found between a person's legs. In fact, you need to travel a lot further north than that. Thanks to countless scientific studies, it is now generally accepted that the brain plays the biggest part in conjuring sexual pleasure rather than physical sensation alone. A rather important distinction for those of us interested in creating fiction in which the sex scenes seem as vivid as any other episode depicted.

THE MOST IMPORTANT SEXUAL ORGAN

The question is: how can we use the fact that the brain is the most important sexual organ to enhance our writing?

One of the challenges of writing sex is that it can be a physically complicated thing to describe. Especially if our characters are getting adventurous and trying out something specific that has taken a lot of set-up. And your reader, in order to appreciate what your characters are experiencing, does need to know what is physically happening in the scene. This said, a mistake that so many writers make in this genre is to essentially write what amounts to little more than an instruction manual. So often, the reader is clear on where everyone is and what everyone is doing but they have no idea about what the characters think of this situation or how they feel about it. Consequently, the writing is not immersive enough and tends to fall short of engaging the reader in the sexual experience.

One approach to avoiding this trap is to weave the thoughts and feelings of the characters through the physical description, using dialogue or interior monologue. In doing this we offer the reader a point of view to connect to. We also offer them some guidance about how they are meant to feel about what they are reading. Readers take their cues from characters. Thus, until you tell them that the character is finding a great deal of pleasure in having their ankles tied to the headboard with a thick length of rope, they will likely be wary of taking pleasure in it themselves.

This rule, of course, does not just apply to scenes of a sexual nature but all descriptive scenes that we write. How do readers know how to feel about the fact the next chapter is set in New York City? How do readers know how to feel about the strange octagonal box a wizard has just gifted our hero? The answer is, they don't until you offer some emotional context. This is why while physical description can play some part in engaging your reader it cannot offer them everything they need. Readers benefit from expressive direction, which they derive either from the narrator or the characters themselves, so it is prudent to always provide it if we want our writing to be as immersive as it can be.

Take this voyeuristic example from *The Memoirs of Fanny Hill* by John Cleland published in 1749:

... he threw himself upon her, his back being now towards me, I could only take his being ingulphed for granted, by the directions he moved in and the impossibility of missing so staring a mark; and now the bed shook, the curtains rattled so that I could scarce hear the heaves and pantings that accompanied the action, from the beginning to the end; the sound and sight of which thrilled to the very soul of me, and made every vein of my body circulate liquid fires: the emotion grew so violent that it almost intercepted my respiration... Whilst they were in the heat of the action, guided by nature only, I stole my hand up my petticoats, and with my fingers all on fire, seized and yet more inflamed that centre of all my senses: my heart palpitated, as if it would force its way through my bosom: I breathed with pain; I twisted my thighs, squeezed and compressed the lips of that virgin slit, and following mechanically the example of Phoebe's manual operation on it, as far as I could find admission, brought on at last the critical ecstasy, the melting flow into which nature, spent with excess of pleasure, dissolves and dies away.

Though undoubtedly over-written in places by modern-day standards, this is still a successful piece of sex writing and it succeeds largely by leveraging the most private observations of the central character: Fanny Hill. At times her view of the sex she is witnessing is physically obscured and so instead of a clinical instruction leaflet about what goes where, which most of us learned at school anyway, we are given the details Fanny focuses on to confirm in her own mind that she is secretly witnessing two people engaging in intercourse. The rattling of the curtains. The shaking of the bed. The directions, the rhythms and of course, most crucially to the success of this piece, the bodily and emotional reactions of our accidental voyeur. The fact that the scene arouses the central character so profoundly spurs the same response in the reader.

The question remains then, how do we ensure we are leveraging character perspective when writing a sex scene?

Ultimately, this comes down to how well you know your characters.

It's common writing advice to complete a character questionnaire for all of your central characters before you begin to write a story. Such questionnaires will often include questions about where the character grew up and what their greatest fear is. Rarely however, do they include questions about the character's sexual preferences. Meaning that we start our stories or poems not knowing exactly where our characters stand on the sexual spectrum. This is a rather core piece of information to be missing about a person we are trying to bring to life.

If you are going to write a sex scene, or in fact even if you're not, I very much recommend you taking the character questionnaire down to this level, starting with the following questions:

How would you describe your sexual orientation?

What is the most thrilling sexual experience you've ever had?

What is the worst sexual experience you've ever had?

Do you watch pornography? If so, what are your preferences?

What fantasies arise in your head when you are aroused?

The above questions are a solid starting point for exploring the sexuality of your characters and ensuring you are letting us in on the thoughts and feelings of said characters as the sex scenes unfold. Such knowledge about the players you are directing through your prose, may also dictate their response to certain people and situations even if you don't plan to include scenes of a sexual nature.

If your story is likely to be largely sexual in nature then I recommend completing the lengthy questionnaire provided in *The Erotic Mind* by Jack Morin for each of the characters involved in the narrative. This questionnaire is intricate and probes at the psychology of sexual preference at a much more profound level. If you answer all of the questions from the protagonist's perspective you will be able base each sexual encounter you portray on that character's sense of sexual identity. This will not only make the sex scene feel more authentic to the reader but will also help them sympathise and relate to the characters you are describing.

CHAPTER THREE:
CONSENT

Before we go any further in our discussion of writing about sex, it's important to address in detail the strangely thorny issue of consent. It has always seemed odd to me that this is a complicated area of story-telling, and indeed life, as it should be the most straight forward part. The rule of consent is as follows: don't touch a person without their permission. Ever. Despite its simplicity however, for some reason, it is a concept we find ourselves constantly having to re-explain and re-define.

If you want to include sexual content in your work, consent needs to be your primary concern. The sensitive portrayal of consent is pivotal not only to writing great stories your reader can enjoy but in remaining, at all times, responsible about the stories you choose to tell. Stories are, after all, very powerful things and if we keep telling the same story over and over again it becomes part of our reality. This is all well and good if the story has a positive impact on us but many concerning stories get told about consent, or the lack of. It is highly likely that you will have heard some of the following stories in your lifetime:

She was wearing a short skirt so she deserved it.

He said 'no' but I could tell that he really meant 'yes'.

At first she wasn't interested but I managed to talk her around.

A few drinks loosened him up and then I could do whatever I wanted with him.

Hopefully, we can all agree that none of these are acceptable ways of conducting ourselves in a sexual encounter. That doesn't mean that your character won't come up against these beliefs, and implied actions. But, in a story written for a 21st Century reader, I would expect such beliefs to be held by an antagonist. And I wouldn't expect anyone who held these beliefs to have a happily ever after, or at least not a traditional one. In short, I wouldn't expect the hero of a story to live by such principles. As a general rule, if somebody touches another person without their consent, in the eyes of the reader they are likely to fall into the villainous category. At the very best they will be viewed as unenlightened.

But what about the dominant male hero in a romance novel? I hear you cry. Aren't there lots of romance books out there where the hero doesn't wait for consent before taking what he wants? And aren't those kinds of stories enjoyed by thousands of readers every year?

It's true that traditionally, romance wasn't a great genre when it came to enlightened portrayals of consent. In some cases, the dominant 'alpha' hero took what he wanted of the heroine without bothering to find out how she felt about it first. It was assumed that the hero was irresistible and thus his prey was willing on some level.

Having read quite a number of romance books written in the second half of the 20th Century however, I can also report that there are many authors who 'got it right'. Who made sure that when the dominant hero finally consummated his relationship with the heroine, there was no doubt that it was what she wanted. In some cases, the hero even asks for verbal confirmation or offers the heroine the opportunity to leave if she doesn't want things to progress any further. If you're looking for a slightly more vintage example of a positive portrayal of consent in a historical setting, I can recommend the works of Bobbi Smith. Considering the time in which she was writing, Bobbi Smith was extremely sensitive on this topic.

In terms of what 21st Century readers expect and want on this level, some of you will be pleased to hear there is still space for a dominant alpha male in a romance story. Such stories still sell very well indeed, and are particularly popular with men and women in high-pressure jobs or who feel as though the responsibilities of the household rest squarely on them. For, when it seems like you have no choice but to take control of everything you need doing, what greater fantasy is there that someone will come along and take that burden away? The role of the dominant alpha hero is to make the loneliness of all that pressure disappear and take care of their beloved in the same way such readers normally have to take care of everyone else. Although the alpha character tends to come into his own during moments of sexual intimacy, the attraction of the alpha male to a readership is more multi-layered.

Thus when such characters appear in modern-day stories, the dominant male does not seek to physically dominate their love interest. Instead, they first seek to dominate that person's mind and heart. Seducing them through the tender care they take of them, the reassurance that they won't let anyone or anything hurt them and their focus on pleasing their intended as they themselves long to be pleased. A true dominant would never have to physically force himself on the object of his affection, or seek to. Such characters in the modern context enjoy the challenge of a seduction and tend to get more than they bargained for on an emotional level when the seduction is complete. In short, they often earn the sexual consent of their love interest by taking ownership for their emotional and physical wellbeing before they take ownership of them physically.

Naturally, when writing about sex, you may wish to explore some of the darker elements of that genre. Perhaps your story hinges around a character overcoming sexual abuse or rape. What I've said above about respecting the rules of consent does not prohibit you from exploring that but I do have one very important piece of advice when it comes to handling such topics: don't show us the abuse in real time. Sincerely, I know some movies do it but it feels gratuitous every time. It feels like someone (usually a male scriptwriter or director) is showing that to us for no other reason than because they can. Unless you are writing about non-consent as a fantasy (which I will discuss in more detail shortly),

I genuinely can't think of one valid reason why you would need to include such material in a story. There are so many other ways of making it clear what has happened to the character without putting the reader through that directly. To do so runs the risk of providing deeply unsavoury titilation for readers with perverse intentions.

This book is nothing more than guiding advice from start to finish, based on my own experiences as a writer. Which, of course, means that you don't have to follow the advice I offer. But when it comes to portraying rape or abuse in real time, I would try to find another way. You could tell us about the abuse the character has endured after the fact, indirectly through dialogue or inner monologue, and it would still be heart-wrenching to know that a character had suffered through that experience. Showing us the long-term impact of the encounter, or encounters, on your character is not only more sensitive, it offers a deeper insight into the profound effect such experiences can have on the victims. It offers you the opportunity to explore questions such as: how does a person move on from trauma? What justice is available for victims of such crimes? How does a person who has been victimised by such crimes stop feeling like a victim?

The only question answered by directly showing the abuse is this one: how did the rape happen? We can find other ways to answer that question without putting our readers through that occurrence in real time. If you ignore my advice completely and insist on including a rape scene in your story, a trigger warning must always be provided in the blurb or synopsis to ensure readers who pick up your work know exactly what they're getting into before they turn the first page.

CONSENT

The above guidance does not include the portrayal of erotic games in which both parties are consenting but perhaps pretend not to be. There are many couples who play games like this. Games in which they say 'no' throughout the encounter. Games in which they struggle to get free of their partner even though that is the last thing they want. Games in which they are bound and gagged without any means of escape and merely act as though they want to get away. Of course, you should feel free to explore the various kinks and proclivities of a wide range of characters in your stories. This is just another way in which writers can be more inclusive and represent a wider range of people in their work. But there is one core thing you must get right in any situation where the consent might be unclear: you need to clarify it, asap. That is, you need to find a way of establishing pretty much on line one that both parties are in this situation of their own free will and for their mutual pleasure.

In doing this, you not only set a positive example about how such games should be engaged with in reality, you give your reader permission to enjoy what is about to happen next. If the consent is unclear, many a reader will not be able to engage with the text. They will be concerned that they are reading something that is morally ambiguous at best, morally depraved at worst. Set your readers' minds at rest from the beginning and make sure it's clear everyone in the scene is there willingly.

The one exception to this rule is writers who wish to write erotic stories of non-consent. That is, stories in which one or more of the parties involved in the sexual activity is forced or coerced into taking part, at least initially. If this interests you, you should know that most publishers will not accept stories that contain non-consent elements for all of the reasons outlined in previous paragraphs. If you choose to write this kind of story you will likely find yourself sharing it only with specialist forums and outlets or selling content direct to customers through your website. But, so long as it's handled sensitively, it is possible to still write in this genre responsibly.

The truth is that quite a lot of people like to read stories about non-consent for a variety reasons and none of those readers would condone real-life rape, abuse or coercion. The most common draw to stories of non-consent is that for many being 'forced' to perform sexual acts is a fantasy. It may seem strange on the surface but the motivation behind this can be traced back to deep-seated shame. Some people still feel a great deal of humiliation when it comes to engaging in sexual acts or admitting their sexual preferences. In the world of fantasy however, if somebody forces a character into participating in a sexual act, they can't be blamed for it. The shame is alleviated because someone else is responsible for making them take part.

When writing in this genre it is important to understand the difference between fantasies that people enjoy in their minds and fantasies people want to act out for real. People who fantasise about non-consent do not wish to be forced into participating in sexual acts against their will in reality. It is merely a safe way of exploring more taboo practices in their minds without feeling shame over them. They may have many other fantasies that they would like to play out for real with an understanding partner but being forced into sexual activity is not one of them.

With this in mind, to write responsibly in this genre it is worth including a disclaimer at the beginning of your story which sets out that this is a purely fictional scenario designed to satisfy a fantasy and that you in no way endorse forced sexual activity in reality. If you are interested in writing stories like this, to you it may seem obvious that it is all fantasy but it is prudent to make that point clear for some readers who may not be as good at distinguishing between a fantasy on a page and what can or should happen in a real-life scenario. Ultimately, there is nothing stopping us from writing about any sexual scenario we wish, but if we are going to put it out into the world for other people to consume we must always be aware of our social responsibilities.

Another reason people read non-consent narratives is to see the captive, slave or victim turn the tables on the person who is holding them hostage. Thus, it is possible to write a story which opens with a non-consent scenario and allows the reader to safely enjoy the elements of that fantasy, while also providing a satisfying and liberating conclusion in which the person who forced the sexual contact is in some way overpowered or humiliated by the victim.

Readers who are drawn to these stories often fear that some kind of abuse may befall them in real life and like to explore how they would process and overcome such trauma should they ever find themselves in this situation. The world of fiction can be a safe place to emotionally exorcise inner demons of this kind provided the writer has thought carefully about the structure of their work. It is, naturally, a sad truth that so many people in our society fear sexual abuse, predominantly women. But following the guidelines above it is possible to write a responsible story in the non-consent category that is pure fantasy but enables such people to face their fears.

If you are just starting to explore sex writing, I advise you to stick to the straight and narrow to begin with and only write stories in which consent is clear. Like any rule you want to bend in any craft, it's important to understand the rule inside out before you start to manipulate it. If you have the inclination to explore darker material, you will likely make much more informed and responsible decisions about how to structure such work once you've had more experience in the genre.

CHAPTER FOUR:
HEAT LEVELS

When thinking about how we might write scenes of a sexual nature, it makes sense to look for guidance in the genre that has essentially specialised in such episodes – or the suggestion of them – since its inception: the romance genre. Though you might not be writing a romance story, much can be learned from such narratives in terms of how to manage sexual relationships within your work.

In the romance arena, several different heat levels have been developed over the years to help readers decide what kind of story they prefer and to reduce the chances of them picking up something that will either offend or bore them. There are countless romance books out there, more than any one person could read in a life time and thus readers in this genre – or any other in fact – do not want to waste time on subgenres that won't satisfy. Hence the creation of heat levels.

HEAT LEVELS

Although these heat levels are aimed at the romance market, they can be incredibly useful guidelines when writing in any genre. They are, in essence, a tool to help writers decide how much sex and what kind of sex to include in their story. Understanding these factors will help you strike the right tone in your work and more than likely serve to help you understand the general shape of your story from page one.

Let's run through the individual heat levels in detail so that you can gauge what kind of writing you are most comfortable producing. Perhaps after reviewing these categories, you will also be able to identify some boundaries you'd like to push in future when crafting new stories.

The lowest, and thus tamest, heat level is that of sweet romance. Stories in this category are, as the moniker might suggest, focused on the emotional aspect of the central relationship. The physical aspect fades into the background by comparison and the nature of the love portrayed often resembles quite innocent ideals that revolve around respect and chivalry. Perhaps the most enduring examples in this category are the novels of Jane Austen which are still loved by many today.

Regardless of which heat level you choose for your story, you will need to consider what is going to happen both 'on- screen' and 'off-screen'. On-screen occurrences happen in black and white on the page for the reader to witness. These encounters are shown in detail in order to illicit an emotional response. Off-screen events are those that the reader understands have taken place but do not witness directly.

In the sweet romance subgenre, the reader will likely be witness to some hand-holding, some hugging, some kissing and possibly some suggestive talk – all of which will be euphemistic and teasing rather than serious and explicit. More often than not, sex scenes in this heat category will happen off-screen. This however, is not a hard and fast rule. A sweet romance can sometimes contain a single sex scene in which the central couple celebrate their love for each other. If a sex scene does take place on-screen within this category though, it will always be described in very broad terms. Again, the reader is likely to be subjected to a number of euphemisms or flowery language in a bid to convey the romantic element of the couple's sexual union. Any such descriptions will also focus on the emotional intensity of the experience rather than what is happening on a physical level.

If your preference is to focus on the emotional aspects of relationships, it is therefore still possible to write sex along these lines. It is no less valid an exploration of sex just because the onus is on the emotional component of the connection rather than the physical aspects of the experience. In fact, arguably, most stories containing sex could do with a lot more emotional content than they usually contain so it's an interesting avenue to explore in your craft. This book is designed to give you the confidence and tools to write as explicitly as you may choose. However sometimes we may feel like shifting focus away from the physical in our work to examine a particular emotional quandary conflict or dilemma. The sweet romance genre – or heat level - is perfect for this kind of narrative.

The next rank on the heat level spectrum is that of sensual romance. This category contains all the heart of a sweet romance but the physicality between characters is cranked up a notch. In such stories there will be a lot more touching between the love interests and the characters are less likely to shy away from public shows of affection. There will be more hand holding, clinching, stroking, kissing and there may even be a scene in which the couple take each other's clothes off, usually in a scene that equates physical nakedness with emotional nakedness. Like sweet romance, any sex scenes will be either behind closed doors or very broad-brush. The aim is to create a sensual interpretation of sex rather than a detailed hard line drawing. It's an impressionistic portrayal that again focuses on the emotional elements of a sexual union.

If we take another step up the heat level ladder, we arrive at steamy romance. Again, at this level emotions still play a very important part in the proceedings. The sex takes place in order to serve character and plot development. This time however, once the sex begins there is no fade to black. Nor is there a closing of the bedroom door. The reader follows the characters through the experience usually from start to climactic finish. Through the explicit description on the page, the reader understands everything that is going on physically and everything that is going on emotionally. This is the first heat level at which you are likely to see the naughty words we will discuss in the next chapter.

Most authors who write in the romance genre favour this level because they're able to explore something physical within the setting of a romantic relationship and the sex earns its place on the page by driving forward the story and developing the characterisation. No detail is spared, physically speaking, but it is woven between the thoughts and feelings of the characters in the scene. Even if you write at a heat level above the steamy category, I still whole-heartedly recommend that you include such detail – more on how to do that later. You may explore emotions and thoughts to a lesser degree at the higher heat levels, but a sex scene without any emotion or thought so often falls completely flat. Thus it is always worth including such detail to some extent to afford the reader a more immersive and satisfying experience.

Beyond the steamy category there are two further heat levels left to consider. The first is explicit. In an explicit romance, you would expect to see everything you would find in a steamy romance but the kink level of the sex scenes would be intensified to cater for an audience who enjoy more risqué material. You may also find the emotional ramifications of the scene are downplayed a little bit in order to create more space on the page to engage with the kinkier nature of the sex. For example, in explicit romance you may brush up against a prominent BDSM theme (bondage, discipline, dominance, submission and sadomasochism), the use of sex toys or explicit dirty talk in the exchanges between characters.

In the fifth and final heat level category of erotic romance all bets are off in terms of what you might find in the sex scenes. The erotic romance genre enables the writer to push boundaries and include materials such as multiple and graphic BDSM practices, unusual kinks or fetishes, group sex, and the enjoyment of pornographic material as part of the foreplay, among many other possible sexual acts.

However, as erotic romance is a subgenre of romance rather than straight erotica, readers would still expect an emotional aspect to the journey. At the end of the story they would also expect the characters to either be happy for now or happy ever after. These are elements rarely considered in erotica stories which tend to begin and end with the sexual encounter, depending on the length of the story, and keep the focus on the sexual union rather than other emotional elements. In erotica, the characters might part ways and never see each other again. This outcome would not please readers of the romance genre.

Hopefully, through these explanations, you can see how the different heat levels in the romance category aid readers in selecting the best stories for them depending on how much emotional content they are looking for and how explicit they wish the sex scenes to be. These heat levels can be easily repurposed for any genre you choose to write in. The categories laid out on the preceding pages are essentially a ratio of emotional activity versus physical activity. At the sweet end of the spectrum there is more emotional content than physically explicit content. With erotic romance the amount of physically explicit content is either equal to or greater than the emotional content.

If you are writing a story that involves sex, it is worth considering this ratio. If nothing else, so that you can flag the heat level in the story blurb or cover page. It's important to apprise readers of how much explicit content they can expect from the outset. If you don't make this clear, people searching for a very explicit story may find your work boring if it's more emotionally charged. Conversely, people looking for emotional inspiration might be shocked or dismayed to find sexually explicit material in your story if you don't offer clear guidance on what kind of story you've written.

You may find through the writing of your story that once it is finished, it is different to what you first imagined. You may have thought you were writing a sweet romance only for lots of explicit content to work its way in there over the organic process of redrafting. Alternatively, you may have intended to write something that was explicit and erotic only to discover it wasn't an appropriate fit for the themes you wanted to cover. The end result might be a story that fits more squarely in the sweet heat level category.

By all means, choose a heat level to work to at the beginning of your project but at the end of the editing process, take the time to reassess that heat level so you are certain your work still sits in the bracket you originally intended. Making this assessment at the beginning and at the end of your writing process can help with editorial decisions such as deciding which parts of the story to keep and which to cut. If you're including sexually explicit scenes in your work, the heat level you choose to work at will undoubtedly shape your story as a whole. Thus, having an awareness of this factor is key. Understanding this element of your work will also help you to pitch or market your story to publishers, publications or readers if you are selling direct.

Never a bad thing when you're trying to build a readership!

CHAPTER FIVE:

NAUGHTY WORDS AND HOW TO USE THEM

If you want to write about sex, the odds are you're going to have to get comfortable with using what others might deem 'naughty words'. That is, words that relate to very private parts of a person's body so that the reader knows what is going on. Words that you'd never dream of using round the Sunday dinner table at your Nan's.

When we talk about writing sex, this is usually the bit of the process we think about. Finding words to describe the intimate nooks and appendages on our characters. Though I hope it's evident from this book that there are many more factors to think about than that, this is undoubtedly an element of the genre writers have to grapple with and for many it is the component most likely to make them cringe.

In old-fashioned love stories the sex portion of the proceedings was often left ambiguous for the sake of the dignity of both author and reader. In some books this meant that the bedroom door would close, there'd be a few blank lines on the page and then the story would resume the next day. The reader was left to guess all of the things that took place in the space of those few blank lines. They were given no hints or clues as to the specifics.

In other books flowery and, at times, vague language was used to describe what was happening between the sheets. In volumes written before the 1990s, it wouldn't be out of place to read a sentence such as this one: *in mere moments they knew the warmth of each other and she gasped as he found the centre of her senses.*

While we can make some educated guesses as to what exactly is happening in this moment it's not particularly informative or, for that matter, erotic.

Often, inexperienced writers in this area will go too far the other way and describe the event in clinical terms, like so: *without warning he pushed his sizeable penis into his boyfriend's anus.*

While nobody could accuse this line of being vague for most it won't prove particularly sensual or arousing.

Having ruled out the vague and the clinical then, we have to consider what words we will use when it comes to describing the act of penetration. Assuming, of course, that we intend to include the act of penetration in our work at all.

As suggested by the previous chapter on heat levels, you are under no obligation to fully describe the act of penetration in your story – even if you are writing about sex. Not all forms of sexual contact involve penetration and at any rate, it is possible for a reader to know that two people are having sex without this element. You could, just as John Cleland did, focus on other images that leave the reader in no doubt as to what is going on. One body positioned on top of another. Thighs parted. The clawing at silk sheets. The shaking of the bed. You wouldn't need to tell us that penetration had taken place for us to understand that the likelihood was high.

If you do want to describe the act of penetration however, and I don't think it's something you should shy from if it's appropriate to the tone of your book, careful consideration needs to be given to what words you are going to use. To not consider this factor puts us in danger of writing something laughable rather than stimulating. As a guiding principle, it is best to use the words that your character would use if they were describing it in their diary. The words your character uses will depend on their social class, what time and place they are living in and how comfortable they are talking about sex in general.

By selecting words that your character would use if they were describing the act, the reader will feel as though the scene is being conveyed in the voice of the character they are following rather than some distant narrator. Given how private the act is, this is a much more appropriate approach.

Moreover, the vocabulary choices will also be in keeping with others you've made in the book and thus won't feel out of place or unnatural. When it is well-written, a sex scene does not feel like some big outlandish event but an inevitable part of the narrative. The obvious next step for the story as it unfolds and the next development for the characters on their journey. Using words the characters would not use themselves is almost certain to make such episodes seem conspicuous to the reader and jar with other segments of the story. The net result of this is that the reader will no longer be able to take your writing seriously or will feel disconnected from your characters and their experiences.

If you are short of alternate words to use for intimate body parts, fear not. English lexicographer Jonathon Green has done the hard work for you. His book Green's Dictionary of Slang has been used to create a timeline of slang words for both the penis and vagina in an online tool called TimeGlider. The exact link is provided in the resources section at the back of this book. If you're impatient to get to it, a quick online search will bring up the timeline which is packed full of ideas for the erotic writer, even if your story is taking place in a historical setting.

Alongside the traps of being overly clinical or overly vague, there is one last hazard writers need to be aware of when writing erotic prose or poetry: adjectives. I know, adjectives seem so small and harmless, why should we worry about them? Unlike their cousins, the adverbs, they're supposed to enrich our writing, right? Well, in truth, adjectives are strangely tricky weapons for authors to wield at the best of times. Whether we're describing settings or characters we seem to be hell-bent on using three where one will do. And in a first draft I'm as guilty as anybody else on this. We're so concerned that our meaning is clear to the reader that we have a tendency to over-egg the pudding somewhat. Never is this such a mistake as when writing about sex. If you do fall into this trap you end up with something like this:

He pulled out his extensive, pink, silken, throbbing cock.

This is the kind of writing that comes to mind when people think of bad sex writing. It's over-written and each word seems to be in competition with itself, trying to out-do the last in terms of impact on the reader. As a result all words in the sentence fail and the whole sentence is too distracting for us to take it seriously.

One adjective will do, at most, like so:

He pulled out his throbbing cock.

Or

He pulled out his cock. He wanted her so bad he could feel the throb all the way from root to tip.

While neither of the above sentences would win any awards for literary prowess they are clear, concise and most importantly not overwritten. The writer is not attempting to bombard the reader with as many descriptors as possible. They are just letting one adjective speak for itself and allowing the reader's imagination do the rest. By restricting ourselves in this way, we are leaving space for the reader's interpretation. We are not telling them what to see, we are inviting them to visualise.

NAUGHTY WORDS AND HOW TO USE THEM

If your characters are pretty blunt or forthright, they might say words you would never normally use yourself. And at first it can feel very strange to write these words down in a story. The more you write about sex however, the less uncomfortable it will feel to use 'naughty words'. They will just become part of the vocabulary set you use to tell the best story you can. And just like all the other words you choose to convey meaning to the reader, you will become more experienced at selecting just the right word to have the desired effect.

Like almost any part of the craft, the key is going to be practice. To this end, it is worth experimenting with different words in pieces of work that are for your own eyes only. This way, you can enjoy the process of finding the words you and your characters are most comfortable with without worrying what anyone else will think. You might not hit upon just the right combination of words the first time you have a go at writing an erotic scene. But if you have the courage to practice and learn by your mistakes, I have confidence that you will find a – ahem – rhythm that pleases you.

CHAPTER SIX:

SETTING THE MOOD

As an avid reader of romance novels, old and new, good and bad, I've been exposed to numerous techniques for segueing into sex scenes. Too often however, moments of physical intimacy take me completely off guard. In such cases the author hasn't properly built towards this situation within the story. It's strange because most writers understand the important role foreshadowing has to play in story structure and yet so many sex scenes aren't even hinted at until they're happening. When a story is executed in this way, the sex seems to sort of come out of nowhere and is often in sharp contrast to whatever was happening in the last chapter.

Unfortunately, the net result of this shortcoming, is that it reminds the reader they are engaging with a story. Belief is no longer suspended and the story itself ultimately becomes less immersive.

Every creative choice we make when telling a story is an attempt to lull the reader into the fictive dream. Abrupt changes in tone tend to snap the reader awake, returning them to reality and forcing them to consider whether or not to continue their connection with our characters.

If you are writing pure erotica then tone is often more easily navigated. The tone of an erotica story is usually evident from the very first line in which we would expect a central character to either be in the middle of an explicit sexual encounter or on the brink of embarking on one. There will be no shock moment for the reader when sex suddenly becomes the main agenda because, in such stories, sex is the main agenda from word one.

Other kinds of story, however, require more subtle crafting. Thankfully, there are many ways to weave the idea that intimate contact will happen through your story before it physically takes place.

Your first go-to is your characters' thought process. Or, as it is more officially termed, interior dialogue. Long before the characters lock lips, or bodies, you can present the reader with what the central character thinks is going to happen or what they would like to happen. When you come to write the sex scene, it may not happen exactly as the character had imagined it but introducing the idea of desire will set the mood for whatever does happen later. This also makes it clear that the character is consenting to the union. It is something they want. Something they have fantasized about or at the very least have considered. These are just a few possibilities. What kinds of thoughts your character has will be determined by what kind of physical contact is going to take place later in the story and what role it plays in the character's development.

Beyond that, you can move into dialogue to further foreshadow any sex that might take place later. You could show a character talking to a friend about their desires for their intended. You could write some flirtatious banter between the love interests. You could blend thought and dialogue by having your character insist they are not attracted to the love interest whilst secretly admitting that they are attracted to them but for whatever reason do not believe a physical union possible. Again, this builds on the idea that something physical is likely to happen between these people so that when it does happen it doesn't come as a complete surprise.

Moreover, just because you plan to include sex in your story does not mean it has to go from intense eye contact to penetrative sex with no stops in between. There is a whole spectrum of intimate activities between these two extremes including: hugging, kissing, stroking, groping, fingering, masturbation, dry humping, dirty talk, oral sex, the use of sex toys and the viewing of pornographic material for mutual pleasure. And this is hardly an exhaustive list. But you get the idea. Sex is much more than penetration and your writing should reflect that. Especially if you want to build to a penetrative encounter.

Naturally, the suggestions provided shouldn't be used as a checklist for every story that you write that involves sex. If the characters know each other well, or are strongly attracted to each other for example, they might leap from kissing to penetration. If you are describing a scene in which a prostitute has been engaged, there might be nothing except penetration. Or there might be oral sex and no kissing. It is the writer's responsibility to think carefully about the situation they are presenting and decide what the characters they have created might reasonably do, think and feel. How they might respond to intimate contact under the circumstances.

If you really want to give the reader an opportunity to acclimatize to the rise in heat level, I can recommend building towards the moment of sexual contact and then inserting a chapter break. I regularly use this technique when writing romance stories and it serves the story on a number of levels. Firstly, if I end a chapter just after the characters have kissed and have both signaled they want to take things further, this serves as a terrific prompt for the reader to turn the next page. Hopefully by this point, they are invested in the characters and are intrigued to see where a physical union might take them. So, in short, such a chapter break keeps my reader turning the pages.

But it also does something else very important. It gives the reader a moment to take a breath and prepare for the shift in heat level. If the last lines of one chapter show characters starting on the path of physical intimacy then the reader is more prepared for that thread being picked up again and continued in the next chapter. This breathing space allows the reader an opportunity to adjust and prepare for the intensity that follows.

It is worth noting here that the more build-up you have to penetration, or whichever form of physical intimacy you are depicting, the more tension there

SETTING THE MOOD

will be in the story and the more anticipation there will be from the reader.

I once read an interview with TV script writer Simon Moore in which he described his discovery of URST (unresolved sexual tension). This, he believed, was the key to ensuring viewers always tuned in for the next episode. There is no reason whatsoever why you can't use URST to keep readers turning the pages while writing prose in order to build-up to a climactic physical moment between the characters. This kind of foreshadowing, that which affords the writer and the reader the opportunity to explore the various aspects of sexual contact aside from penetration will also serve to prevent you from regurgitating the same tired lines as the writers who have gone before. Historically, sex in mainstream literature has been somewhat one-dimensional and representing the many facets of intimacy will support a more rounded portrayal.

There are, of course, no hard and fast rules when it comes to creative writing. Every rule ever set out can be manipulated for effect and this applies just as much when we are writing about sexual relationships. On the whole however, the worst sex I've read is sex that is not so much as hinted at on previous pages of the story. Sex that seems to have been artificially implanted into the narrative for gratuitous titillation only. Avid readers can spot scenes like this a mile away and they won't thank you for including it.

Just as one might seduce a lover in real life, one has to think about how the reader might be seduced into immersing themselves into whatever sex scene you choose to write. Taking the reader off guard or including sex for the sake of it are not likely to be winning strategies, which leads us neatly into our next topic: how to write meaningful sex.

CHAPTER SEVEN:

MEANINGFUL SEX

Although this book celebrates your right as an author to explore sexual scenarios in your stories, as explained in the last chapter, there is no point whatsoever in crowbarring sex into the narrative for titillation alone. At least, not if you are hoping that readers will connect with your story and the characters in that story.

The question remains then, how do we ensure any sexual content is meaningful to the characters and to the reader? The answer lies in the more general craft of story-telling.

In every work of fiction we turn our hand to, be it poetry, prose or script, we are trying to move two very important components forward: plot and characterization. Sometimes a unit of action will move forward just one of these components but ideally the vast majority of chapters or verses we write will serve to move both forward simultaneously. Sex scenes are no exception to this guideline. Each instance of intimate contact that you present to the reader should tell us more about the characters involved and help the characters develop. Additionally, a sex scene, of any variety, should also serve whatever plot you have cooked up.

Sometimes this granular element of structure can feel quite overwhelming so let's look at each of these components in turn, starting with characterisation. Before writing any sex scene (or indeed any scene at all) consider the following question: how will each character involved in this intimate act change between when the scene starts and when it ends?

Perhaps one of your characters will sleep with another character because they believe they're in love with them. When they become intimate with that person however, they may find that they lack sexual chemistry and that the love they thought they felt was based on nothing more than a fantasy of what it would be like to be with that person. This is not what we would traditionally expect from a story in which two characters begin a sexual relationship. Usually, it is a means of showing how the emotions are developing between two (or more) characters. But though not what we might traditionally expect, this is still a valid shift of perspective for a character after an intense physical experience.

As you can see from the example above the sex scene you write can act as a catalyst for any form of change. Other ideas include a person sleeping with another out of pity and then realising their emotional attachment to the other person goes much deeper than that. Perhaps your character sleeps with another character to enact revenge on someone else, believing it will quench their anger, only to discover they feel empty at the end of the experience. If you do use a sex scene to move the plot forward along more traditional lines i.e. to deepen a relationship between two people who are already attracted to each other, at the end of such episodes we expect a declaration of devotion before some bigger, unforeseen obstacle pushes the two love interests apart. But even in this conventional scenario, the people at the centre of the sexual relationship have experienced an emotional shift as their love for each other has either been confirmed or deepened by the act of physical intimacy.

Ultimately, regardless of how many people are engaged in physical contact or what the circumstances are, the characters cannot be the same coming out of the experience as they were going in if the sex scene is to earn its place on the page. Some realisation or epiphany must come out of it, and the more surprising the better.

Let's now turn our attentions to plot. How can sex move a plot forward? The answer will depend greatly on what kind of story you're telling. Often in thrillers, science-fiction stories and sometimes even in epic fantasy tales, a person who has a sexual relationship with the hero is not destined for a long shelf life. The odds are that the person in question will soon be kidnapped or tortured or killed, or all of the above.

So why show the sex in a case like this?

Isn't it gratuitous?

No.

We have seen these characters bond physically with each other so that we understand the strength of their relationship. The fact that these characters care deeply for each other and have a very fulfilling sexual relationship – and likely an emotional relationship too – only makes the horrors that befall them even more tragic. It also serves to help us to understand at a deeper level any retaliation the hero takes. In essence, showing characters in blissful union with another only to have them torn apart provides strong motivation in plot-driven narratives.

In character-driven narratives such as literary, romance, comedy, mystery or suspense stories, the ways in which the sex scenes drive your plot will largely depend on the character's motivation for entering into that union in the first place. Are they sleeping with this person for a bet? Did they hire a prostitute with a heart of gold because they needed someone, anyone, to connect with? Were they paid by some big crime boss to carry out this intimate contact? Are they drunk and feeling lonely? Are they trying to live a more spontaneous life? Does the person they're sleeping with remind them of somebody else they loved? The list goes on. There are many reasons people might engage in physical contact besides just being attracted to another person. Writing sex enables you to delve into that intricate psychology and use it to tell stories that will, hopefully, delight readers, while also enabling them to explore their own intimate interior life.

Your characters may not fall in love. They may not live happily ever after. But the sexual situations you choose to present to the reader during the course of the story still need to be meaningful in their own right. Otherwise we run the risk of the action on the page seeming frivolous, unnecessary unauthentic and in the worst cases possibly even boring.

Make the interaction earn its place on the page however, and such intimate exchanges will only drag your reader deeper into the complex relationships you are portraying and drive them to keep turning the pages.

CHAPTER EIGHT:
WHAT IS SEXY?

When writing sex it's important to remember that tastes in terms of what is attractive are as varied as the number of people on the planet. It's true that the pornography industry would like us to believe that every single person in the world wants to hook up with a bronzed / bleach blonde / perfectly proportioned / Adonis / goddess with abs and buns of steel. A person who never has a single hair out of place (anywhere on their body) and whose make- up will always stay on regardless of how much they sweat.

In reality however, there numerous attributes that can attract one person to another. Sometimes a person's talent for making us laugh increases the level of attraction. Sometimes it's a person's ability to outwit us or a simple act of kindness. At other times it is a person's eyes, mouth, arms, smile, bone structure or curves that can make them seem irresistible, even if they do not fit the conventional idea of attractive. In fact, it is often the things that make a person a non-conventional beauty that attract our attention. A detail that marks that person out as different; that makes them stand out in the crowd.

Similarly there are lots of different things that can turn a person off, and they may not be the most obvious of things. I once wrote a scene in which my hero kissed the instep of my heroine's foot and an editor asked me to remove it. She explained that anything involving feet is a huge turn off for many people. I was sad to remove this part of the scene because I think that people are unnecessarily disgusted and abashed about their feet. To my mind, it was nice to represent a slightly different view of them; to cast feet in a more positive and sensuous light. The kissing of the heroine's feet also felt like quite a humble act for her partner. A small gesture that suggested the worship or admiration of the heroine.

All this said, I did follow my editor's advice in this instance and it was the right decision. Firstly, because it was a mystery story rather than a romance story and thus the bedroom scenes took secondary importance behind those that focused on solving the crime. A reader may not be expecting to pick up a murder mystery novel and find foot-kissing in it and I wouldn't want a reader to find themselves suddenly reading material they weren't expecting, as outlined in my chapter on setting the mood.

Secondly, I removed this part of the story because I think my editor was right: feet are a huge turn off for a large number of people. Although I would like to change that so that people don't go around thinking of their feet as disgusting appendages they'd rather be without, I don't think that a murder mystery story is the place to try and challenge that view. One day, I will likely find another forum to tackle the feet-kissing issue, but the forum I chose wasn't appropriate because I hadn't taken the likely tastes of the readership into account. If I had been writing a literary story or perhaps even an edgy spy-thriller I probably would have kept the foot kissing. But I wasn't. And so that creative choice was saved for a more suitable project, with more suitable characters. You can't predict everyone's tastes but there are some things that, unless you're catering for a particular market, it makes sense to run past an editor to make sure it's a fit for your story.

When writing sex scenes in which at least one of the parties involved is attracted to the other it is important to zoom in on those idiosyncrasies that make the partnership pleasurable and provide tangible detail. There is little point, for example, in telling the reader that a character is pretty or handsome if you're trying to convey a deep sexual attraction. Pretty and handsome mean something different to everybody. If you tell us however that a character has eyes that are ice blue, the colour of the North Sea on a winter's day, we understand that this person has a striking quality to their eyes. And even if we personally prefer brown eyes or green eyes in the partners we choose, we can understand, and empathise with, the attraction the character feels. Because many of us, if we're lucky, have experienced a moment in which we look into somebody's eyes and we see something extraordinary there that perhaps others cannot see. By being more descriptive and specific you are allowing the reader to understand and engage with the attraction between your characters at a deeper level.

When your characters' clothes come off the same rule applies. Be specific about what your character finds attractive in another and be brave about the kind of body types you choose to include in your stories. Not everyone has to be, or even should be, a muscled gym bunny with not an ounce of fat on them. Your reader probably won't look like that. So why not help people with different body types appreciate the attractiveness of their own body and see themselves represented in fiction?

I have received the odd comment in the review box here and there for daring to include a romantic hero with a round stomach in my stories, rather than a man with washboard abs. But on the whole you'll find your readership welcome individuality, certainly mine has. The more individual a character, the easier they are to visualise and connect with. Especially if their physical idiosyncrasies might be considered flaws by some. Remember, the reader is a flawed human being too and although it's nice to read about conventionally good-looking people finding a sexual parter that really sets them alight, it's arguably far more engaging to read about a less conventionally beautiful person finding romantic and sexual fulfillment because the characters are more relatable. In short, there's a reason why *Dirty Dancing* has proven a timeless, undying hit at the box office. Jennifer Grey's character 'Baby' is ultra-relatable to a lot of women out there.

If you'd like to do research about the different body types, shapes and configurations out there, I can recommend looking into the body positivity movement. Numerous articles and countless images can be found online under this umbrella term so it's a good place to start the search for inspiration. That said, being more inclusive about body shape is a lot more straightforward than most writers seem to realise.

For example, one of your characters might have a more rounded backside that they are somewhat self-conscious about. And perhaps that rounded backside is sexy to the other person in the partnership either because they simply have a kink for that body shape or because it betrays their humanity, implies their love for food or their unwillingness to let beauty standards dictate how they live their life. Perhaps your character has scars on their body. Perhaps they are thinner in places where society dictates they should be broad and muscled. Perhaps they are shorter than they would like but their partner notes that when you're horizontal height isn't so much of a consideration.

The inclination of many writers who add sex scenes to their stories is to only write about people who might appear on the cover of a magazine. People who live up to the unrealistic physical beauty standards expected of us. When writers make this creative choice they can quickly alienate the reader who more than likely won't have the means or the inclination to sculpt their faces and bodies in this way.

Beyond this, the writer is squandering an opportunity to be more representative. For example, sex scenes between able bodied people and people managing a disability are quite rare in literature. People who are managing a disability are often cut out from this kind of story and it is a deep shame that we don't celebrate different kinds of bodies and their capabilities when the bedroom door closes (a strong filmic example is the movie *Coming Home* starring Jane Fonda and John Voight).

By thinking along less conventional lines when we consider what a character might find attractive in another, we create more inclusive and authentic work. And here's a big secret people don't talk about much: vulnerability is considered by many to be a very sexy quality and physical flaws can serve as an outward emblem of this. It is a comfort to know that the person we're being intimate with isn't perfect, just as we are not perfect. It gives us a chance of feeling worthy of them. This is an element often overlooked by writers creating sex scenes and is something that could so easily add real depth to their work.

CHAPTER NINE:
REWRITING SEX

Traditionally, sex scenes in literature have taken place between one man and one woman, reinforcing the heteronormative view that society has favoured for centuries. Within those sex scenes, the man has often been dominant and the woman submissive. This is still a highly popular way in which to write a sex scene and shouldn't be disparaged just because it's traditional.

This might be exactly the sex scene you had in mind when you picked up this book and it might be the only kind of sex scene you feel comfortable writing. This is of course all perfectly fine. You are free to write what you wish to write and there are still many interesting ways to execute such a scene and the advice that follows in this chapter will still be of use to you.

Beyond the heteronormative sex scene however, there are lots of other possible scenarios to explore when writing about sexual relationships. These include homosexual, fetish and group sex encounters. Should this be material the writer is comfortable to explore, they should not feel limited by what has gone before but rather seek to open up the page to new kinds of union and celebrate all expressions of intimacy. This is essentially what it means to embrace sex positivity in your work at every possible level.

Regardless of the kind of sex scene you might be writing, traditional or progressive, there is one crucial factor I would recommend exploring: the role of masculinity and femininity within the episode portrayed. Masculine energy may not be coming from a man. It may be coming from a woman or a person who identifies as trans or non-binary. Likewise the feminine energy may not be coming from a woman.

Some people find great liberation in the reinforcement of traditional masculine feminine roles between the dominant male and submissive female. But just as many people find sexual liberation from shedding those traditional roles and being able to engage in more fluid behaviour, bucking the expectations that have been placed upon them by society and disassociating their sexual experiences from the pressures of everyday life. There is often such a burden to behave in a certain manner outside the bedroom that an incredible release can be achieved by removing such expectations inside the bedroom.

Before you start writing a sex scene, think carefully about where the masculine and feminine energy is coming from in this situation and how it will be expressed. It could be as simple as a woman taking charge of the situation, being the person who initiates the contact or the person who controls what kind of sexual contact takes place. It might also be a scene in which a man wears a woman's clothing or has his toenails painted. Or in which a character who identifies as trans fully embraces the energy of whichever gender they have transitioned to. In such cases the erotic charge in the scene comes from the transgressive behaviour. The sense that these characters are engaging in an act of sexual rebellion or unapologetic empowerment that would be frowned upon by their social peers. Because they have found a partner (or partners) that they trust, they are able to become somebody different to the person they project in all other areas of their lives and are able to express something profound about who they are. Something that perhaps they don't get any other opportunities to express, except during sexual situations.

When writing a sex scene, I encourage you to embrace the idea that the characters are not bound by the typical expectations of their gender – so far as this fits the story and the characters you have created. Instead, write as though any party involved in the intimate contact can do anything they wish, so long as they have consent for it. Give them an opportunity to challenge traditional thinking about how men, women, trans and non-binary individuals experience intimacy. This includes the idea that sex is only physical for men rather than emotional experience. Or that for women sex is only an emotional experience and their interest in purely physical pleasure is limited. Or perhaps you'd like to bust some of the deeply damaging myths about transgender people? Sadly, there are many to choose from.

There is much work to do on all fronts.

So whenever you can, I encourage you to allow your male characters to express vulnerability. Allow your female characters to act hedonistically or aggressively. Allow your non-binary characters to embrace behaviours they feel most comfortable embracing without being bound to whatever body they were born into.

By engaging with this advice, you will not only write more inventive sex scenes. You will come to understand the psychology behind a range of sexual practices and what draws people to them. You will have the opportunity to inform a reader of these things too, broadening the horizons of your readership when it comes to what is possible and acceptable in the bedroom.

In reality, people are opening up to the idea that they don't have to experience something like sex on only one traditional plane. People are becoming more open and experimental. As writers of this kind of material, it is prudent to ensure we are writing stories that are in line with the current view but also, perhaps, are leading the way a little bit. Spurring people on to be open-minded about the kind of sexual experiences they might engage in or find pleasure in through the stories they read. The stories we consume do have an impact on us. Often people dwell on the negative impact stories can have but encouraging people to embrace all aspects of who they are, whether they would be accepted in a traditional setting or not, is just one way in which we can do good through our stories. Through our work we can help the less visible members of society feel seen and accepted. This kind of approach also helps to support more accepting. In the long run, there are very few things more important than that.

CHAPTER TEN:

WORKING WITH THE SENSES

We've already acknowledged that it's important to take some steps when writing about sex to prevent it from feeling like a clinical instruction manual. My primary suggestion to avoid this outcome is to weave thoughts and feelings through the physical details of any sexual encounter to ensure the description is more immersive. There is however another method that can pay dividends if it's used sparingly and selectively when describing a sex scene and that is working with the senses.

Before we look at how we can include sensory imagery in our sex writing, this seems like a good juncture to take a step back from sexual encounters and acknowledge something glaring about the process: objectively speaking, sex is a pretty ludicrous act. As adults we have sort of just come to accept how silly it looks and is because we have come to understand it as a doorway to things we want: greater intimacy with another person; a child; mind-blowing pleasure. But most kids who are told what sex entails at a young enough age will tell you straight: it's a very stupid idea.

Certainly, this was how I felt at the age of eight when, after I asked, my mother first broke the news about how babies were made. I remember looking at her as though she was insane and part of me wondered, given that she is a notorious wind-up merchant, whether her explanation was a cruel joke. Who in their right mind would ever think that was a good idea? My pre-teen brain simply could not process such an abominable act. Thankfully for her self-esteem as a parent, I think my poor mother found my reaction quite entertaining. For the next few hours I veered between utter revulsion and disbelief that adults could possibly be interested in doing something so weird. Eventually I pacified myself with the fact that I would solve the problem right then by taking a vow never, ever, ever to do that. Ever. If they wanted to, everyone could play their silly game.

But not me.

No way.

It may not come as much of a surprise at this stage in the book that my vow of celibacy didn't stick.

Why am I sharing this personal anecdote? I promise there is a sound rationale. In essence, it highlights the problem with bad sex writing: it reminds us that sex is a ludicrous act. That if aliens landed on earth and asked how we procreated we might be a bit embarrassed to tell them. Or have difficulty in explaining exactly how people's bodies fit together in that way. Most of us would certainly rather not draw them a diagram and their likely response, let's face it, would be somewhere between pity and distaste.

When we're writing about sexual encounters, we need to help the reader forget that it's a bit of an odd thing to do with another human being. Rather than the weird physical position, we need to focus on the elements that are seductive and arousing. The way in which our senses are set on fire by such an experience. In short, we need to remind people about why they keep engaging with this strange ritual. What makes it satisfying?

So often when we are writing, not just about sex but about anything at all really, we focus on the visual elements of a scene. A sexual experience however is much more than just the sight of somebody else being physically close to you. It is smells, touches, tastes and sounds, and in order to fully capture an encounter between characters it is important to use some of this detail to make our writing more engrossing.

This advice is most often given to writers when they are describing a setting. A writer is frequently encouraged to think about the different ways in which a location stimulates our senses to help the reader fully engage with the locations in their story. The same advice can be administered when describing sexual intimacy.

Now, before you speed off to write a scene in which all five senses are present in every single paragraph, let me just ask you to hold fire while we discuss this approach in a little more detail. Using the senses in your writing can really make it come alive. With a few carefully-chosen examples your reader can feel as though they're sharing the exact same experiences as your character. But the key phrase of importance here is 'carefully-chosen'. If you go overboard and include all five senses at every opportunity, just as it would with any over-used technique, the impact would be lost.

Remember the troublesome adjectives from the chapter on 'naughty words'? The same 'less is more' principle applies here. In this instance, such overload takes on the quality of a checkbox activity for both you and the reader. Truly, there is no need to use all of the senses in every paragraph and if you do it can feel like an unwelcome bombardment. More of an assault on the senses than a sensitively orchestrated seduction.

Instead, I recommend selecting perhaps two senses to target in each paragraph. This isn't a hard and fast rule, it's a starting point to work from. You may choose to remove one or add an extra one depending on how your work reads. When describing a sexual encounter, there are lots of elements for the writer to pick on. Perhaps you could describe the taste of a character's lips when they are kissed. Our mouths do end up tasting of various things throughout the day, be it our toothpaste, breath mints, coffee, whiskey, and the list goes on. If, for whatever reason, the person we are kissing tastes good that can add another alluring dimension to the kiss and intensify the feelings it provokes.

You might team this with how the character smells. Perhaps there are certain flowers used in their perfume. Perhaps they live by the sea and consequently have a fresh, salty smell about them. Perhaps they bathe in rose oil every night. Perhaps the smell of one character's sweat reminds their partner of a pleasurable memory. Whatever you choose, weaving such detail into the description, alongside the emotional and intellectual content, will offer the reader the most rounded possible portrait of that encounter.

When writing about a sensual experience such as a sexual encounter, it perhaps seems obvious that we should include sensory content and yet it is overlooked by so many writers. And in so doing, they essentially miss an opportunity to get their readers to invest more deeply in their story.

To leave out sensory detail is not only to leave the erotic description somewhat wanting but it is also a missed opportunity when it comes to characterisation. Describing a character in terms of the sensory stimuli they provide and respond to gives the reader a very clear picture of who that character is at their core. Especially if the sensory stimuli in question triggers a particular memory, fear or hope within them. It is perfectly acceptable to add a couple of lines in a sex scene to explain what that smell or taste reminds the characters of. Some might argue that this detracts from the physical encounter but in fact it is likely to intensify it as the emotional significance of the union will be made more obvious to the reader.

Often creative writing tutors will teach their students to show not tell when they construct a story. Although, as outlined in my book: *How to Write Page-Turning Fiction*, I think there is space to both show and tell in stories, the use of sensory imagery in an erotic scene is a golden opportunity to show what is happening in the scene at a deeper level, while also developing character in a neat and concise manner.

If you find ways to entwine the physical act you are describing with the emotional response and the sensory response you will have all of the ingredients you need to create a sex scene your readers will never forget.

CHAPTER ELEVEN:

THE ROLE OF SETTING

It is a generally accepted view amongst the creative writing community that there are three main components to telling stories: character, plot and setting. As one of those writers who likes to keep the craft simple and straightforward, I agree that these are the major components of story-telling with elements like tone, perspective, language and theme weaving through them.

The significance of sex scenes with regards to plot and characterisation have already been addressed in this volume but it is necessary to also address the role of setting in a sex scene.

Given that we are, all of us, writing for a 21st century readership who are very much used to filmic story-

THE ROLE OF SETTING

telling, I encourage you to get as creative as you can with the setting of your sex scenes. Or, at the very least, use setting to convey something pivotal about that particular relationship.

For example, if you wish to explore a sex life that is flailing and miserable you might set your sex scenes in an average bed in an uninspiring bedroom. And when you're describing the sexual encounters, you would likely fixate on exactly what it is about that room that is uninspiring. Is everything beige? Is it too perfect? Are the throw pillows always squarely arranged and the sheets always freshly pressed? Is your character yearning for something dirtier? Something less restrained or organised?

Hopefully you can see how contriving the setting in this manner adds another layer to the sex scene? The environment is as uninspiring as the sex, in fact the characters' surroundings are an emblem of how uninspiring the relationship has become. Though this won't make for the most startling visual in a genre fiction piece it would work quite well in a piece of literary fiction about a difficult or strained sexual relationship. Especially if you later contrasted it with more exotic locations as your character begins to experiment more with their sexuality.

In contrast then, if you are writing a story that is squarely focused on wild, passionate lovemaking designed to thrill the characters, and by proxy the reader, it's worthwhile trying to think outside the usual parameters in terms of where the encounter might take place. At the tame end of the spectrum, you've got cars and lavish hotels to play with but if you wanted to get more adventurous you could choose a secluded cove at a beach. Or a deserted stretch of forest land. Obviously if you're writing explicit or erotic romance you can get much bolder with your choices and move onto shop windows, seedy bars, sex clubs or in the case of Erica Jong's work in front of the altar at church.

On the outskirts of Atlantic City, New Jersey, there is a six storey elephant made of wood and tin named Lucy. She was, in her heyday, a seaside novelty that people would visit and photograph. She is now a museum. I visited this rather unique example of American architecture a few years back and made copious notes on the sensory elements of my visit. I knew I would use this elephant in a story at some point, I just didn't know when, or how.

In my second romance novel, one of my characters pays off the guy at the entrance of the attraction so he can spend some time alone with his girlfriend. They end up having sex there. Yes, in a giant tin elephant by the sea. The scene worked better than I could have imagined because the setting was just like the couple, a little bit weird and kooky but quite cute and lovable when it comes down to it.

I encourage you to always be on the search for your Lucy. The more vivid you can make the backdrop to any sexual encounter, the stronger the visualisation in your readers' mind.

Some might, of course, question how realistic it is for two people to have sex in a giant tin elephant by the sea. But let me tell you something, my readers didn't care whether it was a realistic proposition or not. Because the scene was grounded in the sensory elements and the truthful thoughts and emotions of the characters, they felt it a charming moment in the book and didn't comment on the level of realism at all. This, I think, is a testament as to how far you can suspend the belief of your readers if the

THE ROLE OF SETTING

other guidelines in this book are followed closely. Rooting any scene – sexual or not – in a character's thoughts, feelings and sensory experience is a promising starting point for drawing your reader into the moment.

And unless you are tackling an autobiographical project in which you are beholden to the truth (which is arguably the bravest way to write about sex as you are laying yourself quite literally bare on the page), it's important to remember that as fiction writers we have given ourselves permission to manipulate the truth as far as we wish in order to create the most satisfying story.

Realism, especially when it comes to sex, isn't always satisfying. And if I can write a sex scene in a giant tin elephant by the sea, then truly almost anything is possible for you and your characters.

CHAPTER TWELVE:

ARE PENNAMES WORTH IT?

If, having read this book, you are still not convinced you can overcome the shame of writing sex scenes, you may wish to consider adopting a penname. People interested in this path sometimes feel that they lack the confidence to write to their desired heat level under their real name. Or are of the opinion that shame will hold them back from exploring the genre openly and honestly. If it appeals, you will have your own reasons and certainly it's a viable option for many: there are many high-hitting erotica authors using a nom de plume.

Pennames are very easy to set up. They appear on your books but not on your financial information so regardless of how you publish your work it is very straightforward indeed to make sure that the money reaches the right person without any hitches – just make sure that there isn't already an author out there operating under the name Princess Consuela Bananahammock first. As long as your penname is unique – or at the very least unique in your genre – the process should be a simple one.

Creating a penname essentially enables you to generate a secret identity that gives you the freedom to explore whatever saucy scenario you want to on the page without worrying about what people will think.

I know, it sounds like the best of all possible worlds, doesn't it?

Before you decide to go down this route however there are some important possible consequences of this choice that you must consider.

Firstly, you will need to make peace with the fact that nobody will know you've written the book. Yes, I know that's the point of a penname. And right now you might feel OK about that. But just wait until you have spent months getting your story just right. Wait until you've spent hours perfecting every word and working with editors to make sure the story is as good as it can be. After all that, regardless of any possible embarrassment you might feel over the steamier elements of your work, you might have second thoughts about putting another person's name on the front of what amounts to an incredible achievement.

Not everyone finishes a manuscript. In fact, most people give up about a third of the way through – if they even get that far - so if you've been working on this piece for years you should think long and hard about giving all the credit to a fictional alter ego.

Sure, it might feature some content that will turn your grandma's cheeks red, but if you've put your work through a rigorous editorial process, the odds are you've created something that is pretty good. Maybe even something great. At the very least, something you can be proud of.

And if you're going to go 100% on a pen name you won't be able to tell your friends or your family that you've written it. You could tell them that you've put out some books under a penname but that will likely just make them more determined to go out and try to hunt these books down. If they are persistent enough the odds are that they will uncover your secret identity, possibly by doing something as simple as checking the browsing history on your computer...

I know what you're thinking, I've been writing murder mysteries too long if I think a family member will go to those lengths. Don't kid yourself! When someone's curiosity is piqued, it's surprising what they'll do to get to the truth.

Ultimately, what I'm saying is even if you don't live in a family of super-sleuths, if you adopt a penname for the specific purpose of hiding your identity then you will need to be more secretive than Bruce Wayne and Peter Parker combined.

In the beginning this might seem quite a fun exercise but over time you are likely to find it tiring to constantly have to cover up what you are really writing and the kind of content you're producing. People will get suspicious about the fact that you're always busy writing and yet they never really see the fruits of your labour. Even if you do tell your family that you have a penname and you don't want to discuss what you write, some of your nearest and dearest are likely to be hurt. Most family members are put out if you don't share everything with them from your musings on contemporary art to your inside leg measurement, and to be cut out of such a significant part of your life is bound to sting.

The seemingly simple solution to this, of course, is to write under your given name in a 'more acceptable' genre and choose a separate pen name for the erotic content you produce. This does solve a few of the problems previously flagged. You will be able to talk openly about the fact that you write. Your family and friends will be able to see the product of all the time you spend writing and they will feel as though they are included in your journey.

But even this approach has its drawbacks.

In writing under two different names you are highly likely to double your workload when it comes to marketing and promotion. Now instead of setting up and maintaining one author website, you will probably have to build two. You will also likely wind up managing multiple social media profiles and email accounts, and the list goes on.

And, obviously, if there's one thing the average writer needs it's yet MORE work that isn't writing.

Most authors in the modern-age feel aggrieved as it is that they have to do so much promotion just to make a small splash in the reader pool. Imagine if whatever workload you manage on that front right now doubled. That's a lot of extra graft and that's what you are signing up for when you decide to adopt an additional pen name. It's a big commitment and it shouldn't be entered into lightly.

A further consideration when adopting an additional pen name is that it may end up all being for nothing. You may manage to keep it a secret from your friends and family. You may manage to cope with the double workload across multiple platforms and profiles. But if even one of your books charts well and you experience the cataclysmic success of somebody like E.L. James , you may find that your top secret identity quickly becomes public knowledge. In this scenario, all of your friends and family will be able to associate you with that name and those works anyway, even after all you've done to conceal the truth about your work. Many of them may not be forgiving about the fact you concealed the truth from them in the first place.

All of these issues leave me wondering if we're better off just admitting that we like to write about sex.

I know it's a radical thought but honestly, the reactions to this revelation are never normally anywhere near as outraged as we imagine. Most people are intrigued by this aspect of a story. Certainly that has been the case with my friends and family... though perhaps that's more of a reflection on my friends and family than it is anything else.

In all seriousness, good sex writing isn't that easy to find. So don't underestimate how much being honest about the erotic elements of your stories might work in your favour.

Being upfront about what we're writing is certainly the easiest and most straightforward option in terms of how much work is in it for us.

Despite these risks and drawbacks, you may still wish to go down the route of creating a penname, rationalizing that the odds of you ever becoming that famous or well-known are low, and that's fine. You should take whatever route into this part of the craft you feel most comfortable with but I wouldn't want you to believe that a penname is an easy way out of all the difficulties attached to writing about sex.

Perhaps the most balanced way of operating under a penname is to use it for largely branding purposes. That is, to create a persona that equates with erotic stories. A name that when people see it, they know there are going to be scenes of a sexual nature in that story. Alongside that, you can write under your given name in other genres that feel more comfortable for you. Authors who use a pen name for branding purposes however, do not hide the fact that the two names are one and the same person. They often put both names next to each other on the same website and social media pages to cut down on the workload associated with writing under numerous identities.

This, in truth, is the perfect middle ground I have used with my fiction work. I write cosy mysteries under Helen Cox and separate my steamy romances out under Helen Louise Cox. Naturally, it's not going to take a detective to spot these two authors are one and the same, but it's not supposed to. I'm not trying to hide anything, I'm just trying to make sure that one of my cosy mystery readers doesn't accidentally buy one of my romance books. If my readers choose to buy books across my pennames, that's great but it's also quite unlikely given the genres I write in. Most cosy mystery readers do not want any sex in the story. This, for me, is the most important reason to create a slightly different penname – to ensure readers aren't taken off guard by erotic content. That, I fear, may damage the trust built between author and reader.

You, of course, could create a penname that was quite different from your given name. Different enough that the average person who picks up their book will perhaps never learn your true name unless they go looking for it on your website. In this instance, only people who are deeply interested in the author and are motivated enough to investigate further will learn the truth, alongside any friends and family members who fancy a snoop around your author website.

This strategy provides the author with a little bit of shielding from putting their given name on an explicit piece of work while also protecting them from some big outing party at some distant point in the future when one of their books under the erotic penname hits it big and sells thousands and thousands of copies.

The truth is if you decide to engage with this work then there will always be some challenging areas to navigate. Unfortunately, sex has been considered a taboo subject for so long it is difficult for us to shake the feeling that we are revealing something very private about ourselves when we write about it. But none of the challenges surrounding writing sex are unsurmountable and at the end of the day, whatever questions or provocations come your way, it's important to remember that you are not hurting anyone by exploring intimate relationships in your craft.

On the contrary you are likely to be helping people get closer to the kind of relationship they'd really like to engage with. Even if those relationships exist only in the world of fiction and fantasy.

Author's Note

Dear Reader,

I hope this book has been useful to you. As with all volumes in the Advice to Authors Series, I have written a book I wish had been available when I first started out on my writing career.

If you have any further questions about writing on this topic, I encourage you to reach out to either myself or other authors and find the answers you are looking for. Sex is such a sensitive topic and it is extremely important that we get it as 'right' as we can when exploring it in our work. So, pretty please, with a cherry on top, don't be afraid to ask the difficult questions you need clarification on. You won't be the first or the last person to ask whatever question I have, I assure you.

If you have found this volume informative and useful, I should be very grateful if you would leave a short review or rating so that other writers might feel confident that this book will support them in their craft.

I wish you all the very best with your erotic adventures on the page!

HLC

Further Reading and Resources

The Erotic Mind by Jack Morin

Green's Dictionary of Slang by Jonathon Green

The Joy of Writing Sex by Elizabeth Benedict

The Literary Companion to Sex edited by Fiona Pitt-Kethley

Little Birds Anais Nin

Renegade's Lady Bobbi Smith

Sex and Death by Sarah Hall et al

TimeGlider Tool exploring synonyms for the vagina through time:
http://timeglider.com/timeline/07f47d6b843da763

TimeGlider tool exploring synonyms for the penis through time:
http://timeglider.com/timeline/194b572e19fd461b

Acknowledgements

A huge thank you to my many students and readers who have encouraged me to write this volume. It is a great privilege to be considered a person who has experience and ideas worth passing on to other writers and I can only hope that I have done the topic the justice it deserves.

Heartfelt gratitude is also due to Ann Leander who has provided fantastic editorial guidance throughout the writing of this book. Thanks also to my designer Hammad Khalid, without such support and dedication books such as this one would never be finished.

www.ingramcontent.com/pod-product-compliance
Lightning Source LLC
Chambersburg PA
CBHW071534080526
44588CB00011B/1667